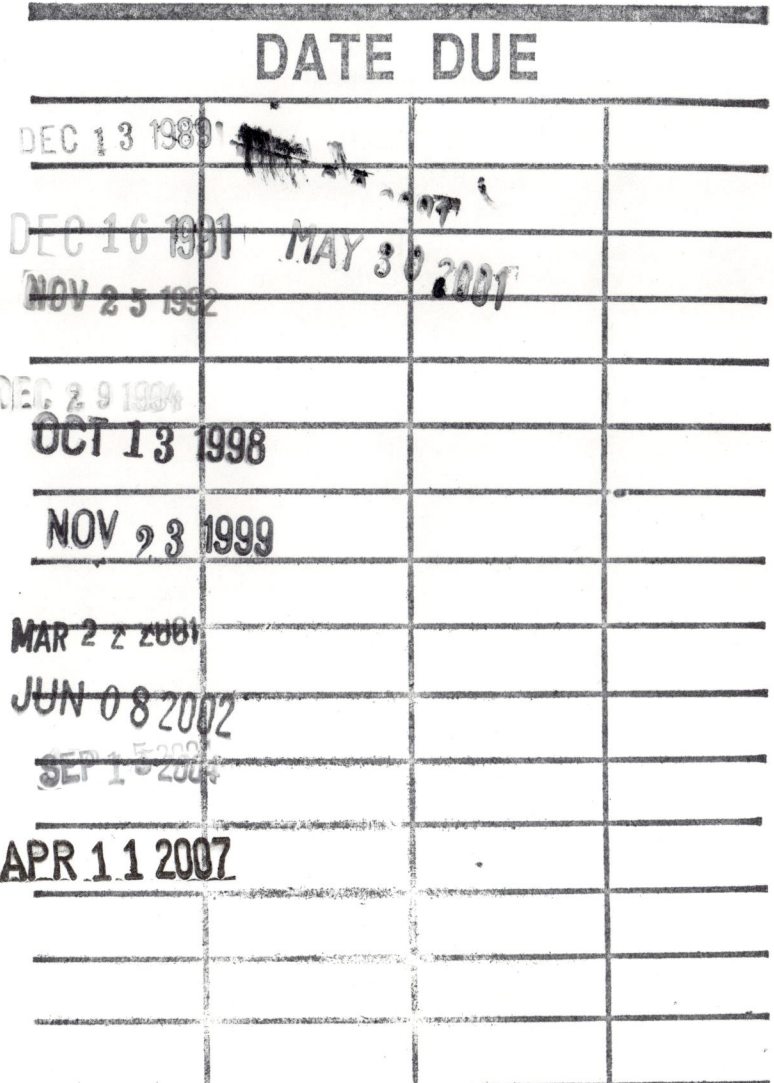

STARRING
FRANCINE & DAVE

STARRING FRANCINE & DAVE

Three One-Act Plays By
RUTH YOUNG

Orchard Books
A DIVISION OF FRANKLIN WATTS, INC.
NEW YORK

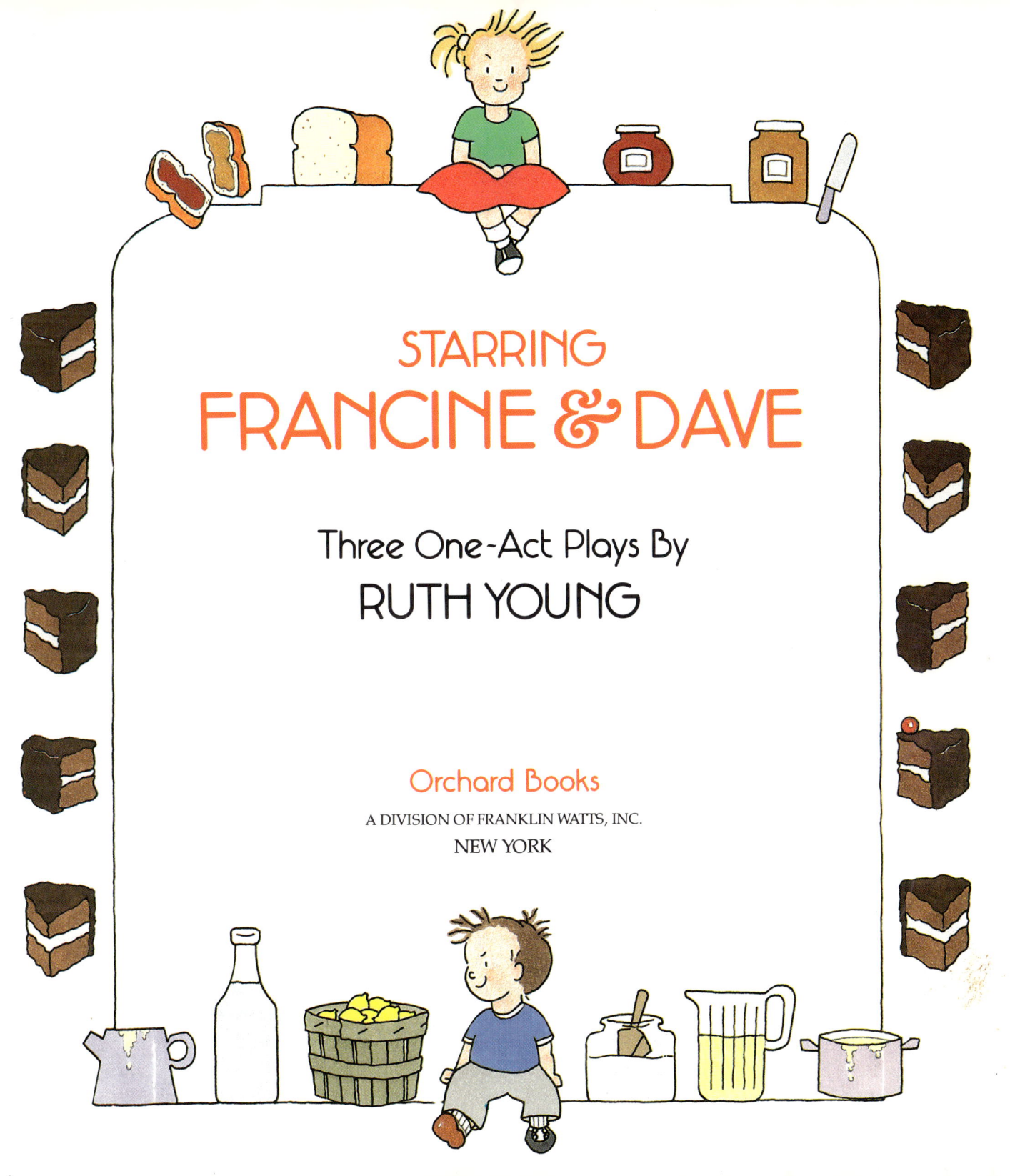

To George

Text and illustrations copyright © 1988 by Ruth Young
All rights reserved. No part of this book may be reproduced or
transmitted in any form or by any means, electronic or mechanical,
including photocopying, recording or by any information
storage or retrieval system, without permission in writing
from the Publisher

Orchard Books
387 Park Avenue South
New York, New York 10016

Orchard Books Canada
20 Torbay Road
Markham, Ontario 23P 1G6

Orchard Books is a division of Franklin Watts, Inc.

The text of this book is set in 12 and 14 point Palatino.
Manufactured in the United States of America.
Book design by Sylvia Frezzolini

10 9 8 7 6 5 4 3 2 1

Library of Congress Cataloging-in-Publication Data
Young, Ruth, 1946-   Starring Francine & Dave.
Contents: Peanut butter and jelly—Lemonade—Chocolate cake.
Summary: In three short plays, Francine and Dave learn to make
peanut butter sandwiches, try to make lemonade, and eat a whole
chocolate cake. 1. Children's plays, American. [1. Food—Drama.
2. Plays]   I. Title.   PS3575.O853S74   1988   812'.54   88-60093
ISBN 0-531-05781-X
ISBN 0-531-08381-0 (lib. bdg.)

Peanut Butter and Jelly
A DISCOVERY IN ONE ACT

STARRING: Francine and Dave
TIME: a Tuesday afternoon after school
PLACE: Dave's mother's kitchen
PROPS: a loaf of bread, peanut butter, jelly, a spreading knife

FRANCINE: Time for a snack! Do you like peanut butter and jelly sandwiches, Dave?

DAVE: I love them! But I've never made one.

FRANCINE: Me neither, but I've eaten a lot of them. Let's see now: peanut butter, jelly, bread, and a spreading knife. There!

DAVE: Now you have to put the peanut butter on, right?

FRANCINE: Right! (*She spreads it over one side of one piece of bread*).

DAVE: Now put the jelly on!

FRANCINE: Right! (*She turns the same piece of bread over and spreads jelly on its other side.*) Hmmmm. What do you think Dave?

DAVE: Something's wrong with that one. Sandwiches have two pieces of bread.

FRANCINE: O.K., I'll start over. I'll spread peanut butter on this piece of bread—

DAVE: And I've got jelly on this old one here! (*He takes the first piece of bread and points to the side already spread with jelly.*)

FRANCINE: I don't think so, Dave. Sandwiches have two pieces of bread but they don't have anything on the outside. Just the inside.

FRANCINE: Oh! Now I've got it! (*She hands Dave the piece with peanut butter on one side and he holds it in his hand. She takes a new piece of bread, spreads jelly on it, and holds it in her hand.*)

FRANCINE: Now! You go to one side of the kitchen and I'll go to the other—
DAVE: Are you sure? (*They walk toward each other.*)

FRANCINE: Absolutely sure! (*Their two pieces of bread meet in a sandwich as the curtain closes.*)

CURTAIN

Lemonade
A RECIPE IN ONE ACT

STARRING: Francine and Dave
TIME: a Sunday morning in summer
PLACE: Dave's front porch
PROPS: lots of lemons, lots of sugar, lots of water, lots of ice cubes, a knife, a stirring spoon, pitchers, pans and pots, two glasses, a fan, an easel, a pencil.

DAVE: It's hot! Are you hot too, Francine?
FRANCINE: Yes, I am. (*Francine fans herself with her fan.*) I am too hot. And I'm too thirsty, too!

DAVE: Let's make lemonade! Here—some lemons, a pitcher, sugar, ice cubes, water, and my big wooden stirring spoon. (*Dave squeezes lemons into the pitcher, adds water and an ice cube, and pours a little out for Francine to taste.*) How's that?

FRANCINE: It's *much* too lemony.

DAVE: I forgot the sugar! (*Dave adds plenty of sugar.*) There! Now how does it taste?

FRANCINE: It's very, very sweet. *Too* sweet.
DAVE: Well, here's more water.
FRANCINE: Now it's not lemony enough.
DAVE: I'll just add these other lemons here. (*Dave adds more lemons and more water. By now the lemonade fills the pitcher and a pot.*) How is it?

FRANCINE: Oh! It's sour! Add some more sugar, quick! (*Francine pretends to faint.*)

DAVE: (*Dave adds more sugar, more water, and all of the ice. There are four containers of lemonade.*) How about now?

FRANCINE: Delicious! Just the way I like it. Lots of lemons and lots of sugar and lots of ice cubes. But I tasted so much I'm not thirsty anymore.

DAVE: What will we do with so much of it?
(*Francine prints a sign that solves the problem.*)

Chocolate Cake

A FANTASY IN ONE ACT

STARRING: Francine and Dave
TIME: a Saturday afternoon
PLACE: Francine's mother's kitchen table.
PROPS: a very large chocolate cake, two plates, two napkins, two forks, a cake knife.

FRANCINE: I love chocolate cake!
DAVE: Me too!

FRANCINE: (*She cuts the cake.*) There! Two pieces!

(*Dave takes the half with the cherry on it.*)
FRANCINE: Wait a minute! You took the big piece!

DAVE: They're both the same. Here, I'll trade you.
(*Dave gives Francine his piece of cake, takes the cherry off it, takes hers, puts the cherry on it, and begins to eat.*)

FRANCINE: Wait a minute! Let me look again!

FRANCINE: (*Francine looks, then cuts the big pieces in half and then in half again.*) There! Now we each have four pieces.

FRANCINE: One for you! (*She takes one of the little pieces and puts it on Dave's plate.*)

DAVE: And one for you!

FRANCINE: And one for you!

DAVE: And one for you!

FRANCINE: And one for you!
DAVE: And one for you!

DAVE: Just one more bite—
FRANCINE: Don't forget the cherry—(*She cuts the cherry in half.*)

FRANCINE: I love chocolate cake!
DAVE: Me too!

CURTAIN

To produce a play of your own, you will need...

STORY – something that happens at a certain time and place
ACTORS – people to play the parts of the characters in the story
DIALOGUE – what the characters say to each other
COSTUMES – what the characters wear
PROPS – the things the characters use during the play
STAGE – a special place where the play is performed
REHEARSALS – going over and over the play until all the actors know their parts
DIRECTOR – someone to be in charge of what happens on the stage during rehearsals
AUDIENCE – people to sit and watch the play

You may also want to have...

TICKETS – something to give the audience that says they can come to the play
INTERMISSION – a break in the middle of the play
ROSES – flowers for the stars after the play
REVIEWS – notes from the audience on how much they liked the play

IMPORTANT: When you are making up a play, remember that every character in it must want something. They don't have to say what it is, but they have to know it themselves. This makes a play exciting. So make sure your characters know what they want.

NOV 8 1989